See the Bubbles

written by Anne Giulieri
photography by Ned Meldrum

Look at the sink.

I can see the bubbles.

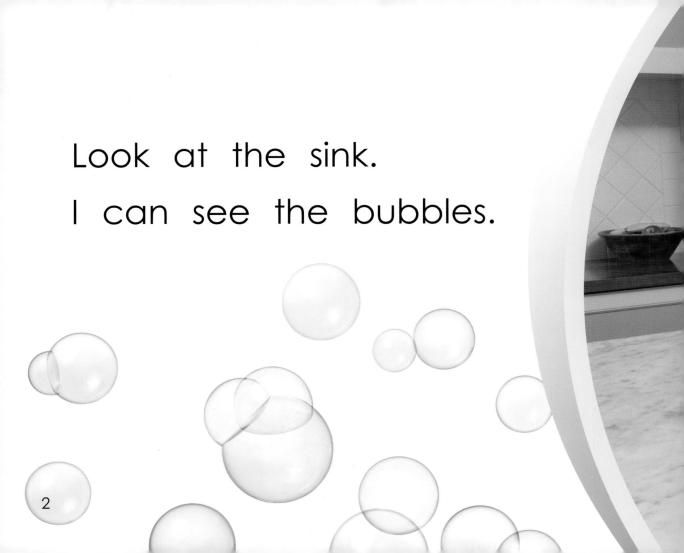

I can play in the bubbles.

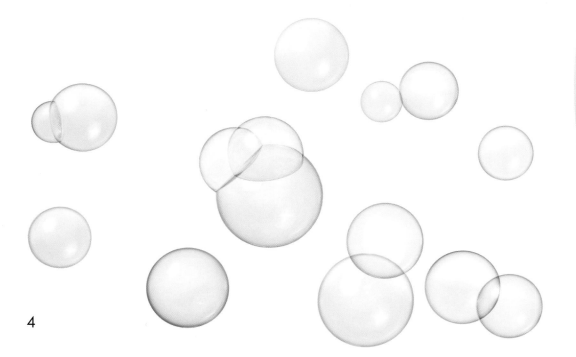

Look at the bucket.

I can see the bubbles.

I can play in the bubbles.

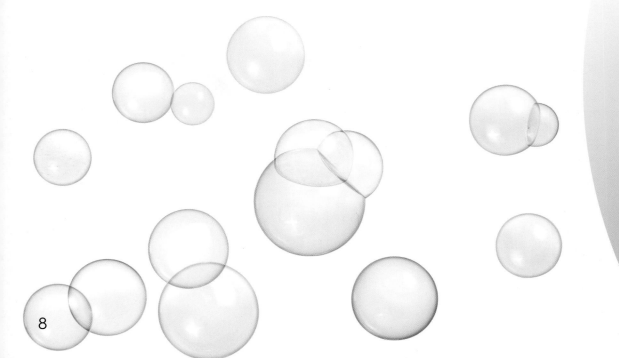

Look at the bathtub.

I can see the bubbles.

I can play in the bubbles.

Look at the clown.
The clown can see the bubbles.

The bubbles
go up and down.